Contents

The First Birdwatcher's Code

Where to look

Start in your own garden – get to know the most common
  birds first

Visit your local park – birds will be easy to see

Visit lakes and rivers – go with an adult: these are good places
  for birds

How to look

Use your eyes – look for birds wherever you go

Use your ears – listen for bird songs and calls

Walk quietly – so the birds don't hear you coming

Stop when you see something – stand, or sit still, and watch

What to wear

Wear warm clothes in winter – birdwatching can be very cold

Wear boots – places where birds live are often wet

Don't wear bright colours – you will frighten the birds

Remember the Country Code

- Don't start fires
- Close gates
- Keep dogs under control (or leave them at home!)
- Stay on the footpath
- Don't climb on fences or walls
- Don't leave litter
- Don't pick or tread on flowers
- Take care on roads and near water

Cormorant

Cormorants are seabirds. They also visit lakes and rivers a long way from the sea. They often stand with wings outstretched. When feeding, they dive and hunt fish underwater.

Great Crested Grebe

This water bird lives on lakes. It eats fish, which it catches by diving under water. In spring, the male and female use their pretty head frills to display to each other. Baby grebes often ride on their parents' backs.

winter

adult–summer

5

Grey Heron

Herons stand very still at the edges of lakes, ponds or rivers so that they can catch fish and frogs to eat. They fold their long necks when they fly. Herons nest together in the tops of trees, in a heronry, just like rooks in a rookery.

adult

juvenile

cygnets

Mute Swan

This is Britain's biggest wild bird. In flight, its wings make a loud 'whooshing' noise. Young swans are known as cygnets. They are pale brown until almost one year old. Swans use their long necks for reaching plants which grow in deep water.

Canada Goose

Geese are larger than ducks. This is the largest of Britain's geese. Canada Geese were brought here from North America over 300 years ago, to look attractive on park lakes.

Many escaped and now nest in lots of places.

male

female

ducklings

Mallard

This is our commonest duck. You will find it even in town parks. The male has bright feathers most of the time. The female is dull brown, so that she is hidden when she sits on her nest.

7

Tufted Duck

The crest of feathers on the back of the male's head gives the Tufted Duck its name. It finds its food (small animals) by diving to the bottom of lakes.

female

male

Kestrel

male

female

Sparrowhawk

Kestrel

This falcon is our commonest bird of prey. Kestrels hunt for mice and voles by hovering. You can often see them doing this beside motorways. Some even nest on buildings in busy towns. **Sparrowhawks** do not hover. They use speed and surprise to catch small birds.

Buzzard

This large bird of prey lives
in hilly or wooded country.
It often sits on roadside
poles or circles high up on
outstretched wings. Its
sharp eyes search for its
meal: a rabbit or some other
small animal.

Red Grouse

Lonely moors are the home of
the Red Grouse. They eat the
tender tips of heather
plants. Grouse never move
far from their moors.
They escape from
foxes, eagles and
other enemies by
hiding among the
heather.

female   male

Pheasant

The colourful male and the drab female spend most of the day on the ground. They sleep in trees at night, safe from foxes. Pheasants were brought to Britain from Russia and China over 900 years ago, to provide food for people. They are still shot for sport.

Moorhen

You can spot a Moorhen by its bright bill and the white under its tail.

They usually bob their heads and tails as they swim on ponds and rivers. You may also see them walk across fields. Moorhens may have three broods of young each year.

Coot

juvenile

adult

The Coot is all-black except for its white bill and forehead (hence the saying 'Bald as a Coot'). On lakes you can see them diving under the water. They eat water plants which they bring to the surface in their bills.

A
COOK

Oystercatcher

Oystercatchers rarely eat oysters, but they do eat other shellfish, especially cockles and mussels. They use their long bills to reach into the mud to find food. They belong to a group of birds called waders because they have long legs, live near water and often wade into it.

Lapwing

The Lapwing was once known as the Peewit because of its "pee-wit" call. In spring you may see its mad, tumbling displays, when its wings make a humming (or lapping) noise. Lapwings gather in flocks in winter.

Black-headed Gull

The dark brown (not black) head is white in winter, with a dark spot behind the eye. It is wrong to call gulls 'sea-gulls', since they are often seen inland. Sometimes, large numbers gather on rubbish tips or behind a tractor ploughing, where they can easily find food.

summer

winter

12

Common Gull

Herring Gull

Herring Gull

This fierce-looking gull has a harsh, laughing call. It is usually seen near the sea. Like other young gulls, juvenile Herring Gulls are brown. The **Common Gull** is commoner inland, but on the coast it is rarer. It is smaller than the Herring Gull and looks more gentle.

Common Tern

This summer visitor is slim and has a forked tail. It catches fish by diving. Common Terns and Arctic Terns look similar. **Arctic Terns** are great migrants: some breed near the North Pole and spend the other half of the year near the South Pole.

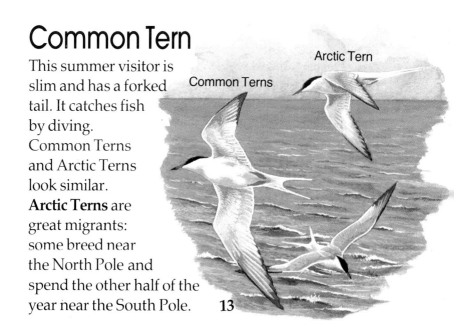
Arctic Tern
Common Terns

13

Puffin

This funny-looking seabird spends the winter out at sea. It returns to rocky islands in the spring. Puffins nest close together in colonies at the top of cliffs. Eggs are laid in holes or in rabbit burrows.

Woodpigeon

Farmers do not like Woodpigeons because they eat crops. In summer you may hear the Woodpigeon's peaceful cooing song and see them swooping up and then gliding down on curved wings as they display. Nests are made from a few twigs and look very unsafe. Woodpigeons may lay eggs at any time of the year.

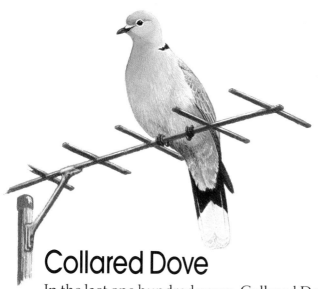

Collared Dove

In the last one hundred years, Collared Doves have
spread all the way across Europe from Turkey. They
nested in Britain for the first time in 1955, but now
they are common almost everywhere.

Rock Dove

Wild Rock Doves are found only on the
coasts of Scotland and Ireland. Hundreds
of years ago, they were kept in
dovecotes to provide people
with fresh meat in winter.
Many escaped and
now live wild. These
are our common
street pigeons.
They can be many
different colours.

adult

Cuckoo

young

Reed Warbler

Cuckoo

Cuckoos do not build nests. Instead, the female lays her eggs in another bird's nest. She usually chooses a Dunnock, a Meadow Pipit or a Reed Warbler. Cuckoos arrive in April, and adults leave again for Africa in July or August. Young may stay until September, when they fly south alone for the winter

Tawny Owl

This bird of the night flies with no noise. It pounces on mice, voles, small birds and even worms. The Tawny Owl's song is a hoot. It also has a sharp "kwik" call. Never go near a nest: owls can be very fierce towards human beings when protecting their young.

Barn Owl

This owl gets its name from its habit of nesting in barns. It also nests in hollow trees. Barn Owls have become rarer. Farmers like them because they eat rats and mice. This beautiful gold-and-white bird can look spooky as it flies silently at night; it also makes weird noises. Many 'ghosts' were probably actually Barn Owls.

Kingfisher

This is a tiny, jewel-like bird. It is usually seen flashing fast and straight over a pond or river. Kingfishers catch small fish by diving. Their nest holes in banks soon smell of rotting fish.

17

Swift

This common summer migrant spends only 15 weeks with us. It arrives in May and leaves during August. Swifts can be seen over towns (where they nest under roofs) and also in the country. Except when at their nests, they fly all the time. They catch flying insects in their wide mouths, and they even sleep in flight.

Great Spotted Woodpecker

Green Woodpecker

The woodpecker's long tongue can reach insects hidden in a tree trunk, or find ants deep in the soil. The Green Woodpecker's song is a shrill laugh. This has given it the country name of 'yaffle'. **Great Spotted Woodpeckers** can often be heard 'drumming' with their bills on a dead branch.

Green Woodpecker **18**

Swallow

Our Swallows spend the
winter in South Africa.
They return to us again
each April. Often
they find their
way back to nest
in the same barn as
the year before. In autumn,
they gather on telephone wires
and bare branches before flying south.

House Martin

This is a relative of the Swallow. It
builds a dish-shaped nest of mud on
buildings. Often, several pairs nest
close together on
houses. To identify a
House Martin, look
for the large white
patch above its tail.
The **Sand Martin**
nests in holes in
banks. It is usually
seen catching insects
in flight over water.

Sand Martins

House Martin

Skylark

This is one of our most common birds. It is at home in open country. It is found everywhere except in town centres and woods. Skylarks sing beautifully as they rise from the ground and almost disappear from sight, high in the sky. Some Skylarks flock together in winter.

Meadow Pipit

In summer, Meadow Pipits are most common on hills and moors. In winter you may see them in many other places as well. Their squeaky call sounds like "seat". Their song is given as they drop from the sky like tiny parachutes.

Wren

This tiny bird has a very loud song. You may hear it at any time of the year. Wrens feed on insects. In winter, if the weather is freezing, lots of Wrens may roost together at night, but many die of hunger and cold. In spring, the male Wren builds several nests and the female chooses one of them.

Pied Wagtail

Pied Wagtails may be seen in towns as well as in the country. They like water, but often visit school playgrounds and places where there is short grass. Sometimes, hundreds come together on winter evenings to sleep in trees, bushes, reedbeds or even buildings.

Dunnock

This common, small brown bird is sometimes thought to be
a sparrow. It is not a sparrow and belongs to a quite different
family of birds. Notice its thin bill: it feeds on insects and
small seeds which it finds on the ground. Dunnocks often
live in gardens.

Robin

Male and female Robins look the same. The male sings all
through the year. His song warns other Robins to keep
away from the place where he
has chosen to
nest or will be
spending the
winter. The
Robin's red   juvenile
breast feathers
are also used as a   adult
warning. Young
Robins are speckled and
brown, with no red.

22

Song Thrush

Redwing

Song Thrush

Worms, insects, berries and snails are all favourite foods of the Song Thrush. To open snail shells, it picks them up and smashes them on a stone 'anvil'. Another thrush, the **Redwing**, is a winter visitor from northern Europe. You should look for the red under its wings and the pale stripe over its eye.

Fieldfare

Mistle Thrush

Mistle Thrush

This large thrush nests early in the year. It sings in late winter from the very top of tall trees, even in bad weather. This has given the Mistle Thrush its country name of 'Storm-cock'. The **Fieldfare**, another big thrush, is a winter visitor from northern Europe, and is usually seen in flocks.

23

Blackbird

The shape of the Blackbird shows you that it is a member of the thrush family. The smart male Blackbird looks very different from the brown female. In spring and summer, listen for the male singing loudly from a safe perch. This may be a tree, the roof of a house or even a television aerial.

female

male

Chiffchaff

Chiffchaffs are usually the first summer visitors to return to Britain in spring. They can be hard to see. Listen for their "chiff-chaff chiff-chaff-chiff" song. The **Willow Warbler** is also a summer visitor. It looks very much like a Chiffchaff, but its song is quite different: a tinkling trill.

Willow Warbler

Chiffchaff

Goldcrest

This is our smallest
bird. In summer, most
Goldcrests live in pine,
fir, or yew trees. They
build beautiful, tiny
nests of moss and spiders'
webs. In winter, Goldcrests
may be seen almost anywhere. The
orange or yellow crest is not easy to see.

Spotted Flycatcher

This summer visitor is very
good at catching insects in
flight. It snaps them up
after a short chase. It then
returns to its perch. Spotted
Flycatchers are woodland
birds. Sometimes they nest
in country gardens.

25

Long-tailed Tit

This tiny bird has a tail longer than its body. Long-tailed Tits often travel around in flocks. They build beautiful ball-like nests lined with thousands of feathers. The nest is always well protected. It is hidden with moss or lichen and is built in a thorny bush. This is so that enemies do not find it or cannot get to it.

Blue Tit

Hang up peanuts in your garden in winter and Blue Tits will arrive. Blue Tits are woodland birds. They like to nest in holes in trees, but will often use nest-boxes in gardens. A family of baby Blue Tits eats hundreds of caterpillars every day.

Great Tit

This is the largest of the tit family. It often joins Blue Tits to feed on peanuts. Male Great Tits have a wider stripe on their breasts than do females. The much smaller and greyer **Coal Tit** has a white stripe at the back of its head. It often takes nuts and hides them.

Coal Tit

Great Tit

Treecreeper

This bird can be very hard to see. It moves jerkily up tree trunks like a mouse. It uses its long, curved bill for finding insects and spiders in cracks in the bark.

Magpie

The Magpie is a member of the crow family. It lives in some towns as well as in the country. In spring, Magpies eat many eggs. They also eat the young of other birds. Their nests are large, untidy balls of sticks, built in trees or tall bushes.

Carrion Crow

Unlike the Rook, each pair of Carrion Crows nests by itself. In parts of Scotland and in Ireland, it has a grey body and is called the 'Hooded Crow'or'Hoodie'. It eats most kinds of food, including dead animals.

Hooded Crow

Carrion Crow

28

Rook

Rooks build large nests in the tops of tall trees.
These nests are usually in groups
called 'rookeries'. They return
to their rookeries in winter.
The first eggs are laid
before there are
leaves on
the trees.
Sometimes,
Rooks eat farmers'
crops and are shot.

Jackdaw

Jackdaws often join
flocks of Rooks. The
Jackdaw is smaller
and has a grey head
with a black face.
They nest in holes,
in trees, in ruined
buildings, in church
towers and even in
chimneys.

Starling

We all know the Starling. Most of the year it travels around in flocks. In the evenings, thousands may gather together to sleep in roosts. These may be in woods, in reedbeds or on buildings in town centres. The Starling's song often includes very good copies of the calls of other birds.

juvenile

adult

House Sparrow

Tree Sparrow

female

male

House Sparrow

House Sparrows usually live near houses or farms. They eat most kinds of food. They nest in buildings or in trees or bushes. House Sparrows are now found all over the world. The rarer **Tree Sparrow** nests in holes in trees. It joins flocks of other birds in winter.

Chaffinch

female

male

The feathers of the handsome male Chaffinch are brightest in spring. He uses his bright colours to attract a female Chaffinch and to chase away other male Chaffinches. The female is duller. She is harder to see as she sits on her eggs.

female

male

Greenfinch

The large bill of the Greenfinch helps it to open hard seeds. Greenfinches like peanuts. They sometimes join the Blue Tits and Great Tits on our birdfeeders in winter. In spring, male Greenfinches fly like large butterflies as they display over their nesting areas.

Goldfinch

This is one of our prettiest birds. Goldfinches are usually seen in small flocks. They have a bouncy flight and a tinkling call. Their pointed bills can reach the seeds of thistles and other plants. Young Goldfinches do not have red faces.

adults

young

adult

Bullfinch

The fat bill of the Bullfinch is very strong. It is used for opening seeds and nibbling flower buds. The Bullfinch's liking for the buds of fruit trees makes it hated by some farmers and gardeners.

The pink of the male makes him very beautiful. The female and juvenile are duller. Look for the white patch above their black tails.

juvenile

male

female

Yellowhammer

This bunting is a common bird on farmland and in open country. The colourful male often sings from the top of a bush or small tree. Some people say that his song sounds like 'a little bit of bread and no *cheese*'. Do you agree? In winter, Yellowhammers flock together, often with other small birds.

female

male

female

male

Reed Bunting

In spring, the male looks very smart. He has a black head and white collar. His song, however, is just a few squeaky notes. Reed Buntings are common around the edges of lakes and rivers. They can also be seen away from water.

More Ideas for Birdwatchers

Here are some things for you to do

Make your own bird book

Write a list of the birds you have seen in a notebook. Draw pictures of some of them. Write down those birds which visit your garden.

Feed the birds in winter

Between October and April birds need plenty of food to stay alive in cold weather. You can help by throwing out kitchen scraps. You can also buy wild bird food and peanuts and put these out in your garden. Why not build a bird table?

Give birds water

Birds need water in summer and winter for drinking and bathing. Put out a shallow container in your garden or build a small pond. Break the ice on cold winter mornings. In summer make sure the water is topped up every day.

Join a club

The Young Ornithologists' Club is the national club for young people who like birds and other wildlife. It is the junior section of the Royal Society for the Protection of Birds. Find out about its colour magazine, its competitions, projects, local activities and holidays by sending your name and address and a second-class stamp to YOC, The Lodge, Sandy, Bedfordshire SG19 2DL.

Your Own Birdwatcher's Badge!

How many of the birds in this book have you seen? When you have seen more than 30 species you may have a free badge.

List the species on a separate sheet of paper, with the dates when you saw them. Send your list, with your name, address, and a second-class stamp to:

The Young Ornithologists' Club
The Lodge
Sandy
Bedfordshire SG19 2DL

You will then be sent a free birdwatcher's badge.

Great Crested Grebe
Cormorant
Grey Heron
Mute Swan
Canada Goose
Mallard
Tufted Duck
Sparrowhawk
Buzzard
Kestrel
Red Grouse
Pheasant
Moorhen
Coot
Oystercatcher
Lapwing
Black-headed Gull
Common Gull
Herring Gull
Common Tern
Arctic Tern
Puffin
Rock Dove

Woodpigeon
Collared Dove
Cuckoo
Barn Owl
Tawny Owl
Swift
Kingfisher
Green Woodpecker
Great Spotted
  Woodpecker
Skylark
Sand Martin
Swallow
House Martin
Meadow Pipit
Pied Wagtail
Wren
Dunnock
Robin
Blackbird
Fieldfare
Song Thrush
Redwing

Mistle Thrush
Chiffchaff
Willow Warbler
Goldcrest
Spotted Flycatcher
Long-tailed Tit
Coal Tit
Blue Tit
Great Tit
Treecreeper
Magpie
Jackdaw
Rook
Carrion Crow
Starling
House Sparrow
Tree Sparrow
Chaffinch
Greenfinch
Goldfinch
Bullfinch
Yellowhammer
Reed Bunting

Index